Dinosaur Discoveries

By Robert Bell
Illustrated by Peter Barrett

Paul C. Sereno, Consultant
Assistant Professor, University of Chicago

Deinonychus

A GOLDEN BOOK · NEW YORK
Western Publishing Company, Inc., Racine, Wisconsin 53404

Over 150 years ago people were digging in the ground when they came across some old bones. These were not just any old bones. They were the biggest bones anybody had ever seen. And scientists soon found that they were not just big: They came from giant animals that were *different* from any others.

Richard Owen, a scientist, gave this new kind of animal a special name. He called it a dinosaur.

The word *dinosaur* means "terrible lizard" in the Greek language. And Mr. Owen wasn't kidding. When scientists put some of the first dinosaur bones together, they made an animal that stood 15 feet tall, with long sharp claws and giant teeth. It was the most surprising thing they had ever seen and only the first of many dinosaur discoveries to come.

Iguanodon skeleton

Dinosaurs were given their names by the scientists who studied them. Their names are often hard to say, but the scientists didn't make them that way on purpose. All dinosaur names mean something.

Sometimes a dinosaur was named for the place where its bones were found. One dinosaur was named Alamosaurus (al-a-mo-SAWR-us) because its bones were first found in the Alamo mountains.

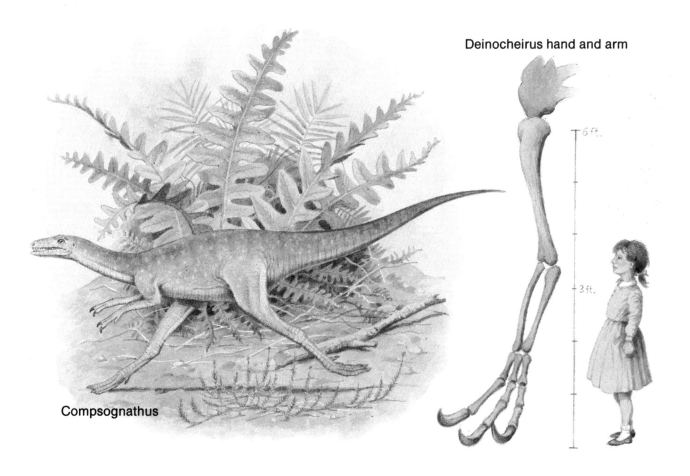

Deinocheirus hand and arm

6 ft.

3 ft.

Compsognathus

Sometimes scientists named dinosaurs for the way their bones looked. Compsognathus (komp-so-NAY-thus) means "pretty jaw," and Deinocheirus (dine-o-KIRE-us) means "terrible hand." Deinocheirus had huge hands with claws that were a foot long.

And sometimes dinosaurs were named for the way scientists think they lived. Saltopus (SALT-o-pus) was named "leaping foot" because scientists think it could run and jump very fast.

Saltopus

Ornitholestes

When someone says "dinosaur," the first thing we think of is a huge, heavy creature. But dinosaurs came in all shapes and sizes. Ornitholestes (or-nith-o-LESS-teez), for example, was about the size of a person. Its name means "bird robber," because we think it hunted birds and other small animals. Small as it was, Ornitholestes was much bigger than Saltopus, a meat-eating dinosaur that weighed only two pounds. Remember "pretty-jawed" Compsognathus? It was no bigger than a chicken, and it probably hunted small lizards for food.

The smallest bones ever found belonged to a
baby dinosaur. Because of the shape of its
mouth, scientists named it Psittacosaurus
(sit-a-ko-SAWR-us), which means "parrot lizard."
This baby dinosaur was no bigger than a small bird.

Brachiosaurus

Brontosaurus

Some dinosaurs ate only meat. Some ate only plants. And even though you might think the meat-eaters were bigger and stronger, the plant-eaters were the biggest dinosaurs.

Brontosaurus (bront-o-SAWR-us) and Diplodocus (dip-lo-DOC-us) grew to be 90 feet long from head to tail. Brachiosaurus (brack-e-o-SAWR-us) was even bigger. And the biggest of all was Ultrasaurus (ul-truh-SAWR-us), which grew to be 100 feet long and may have weighed 200,000 pounds (that's about as much as you and 6,000 of your closest friends would weigh together).

Brachiosaurus

Diplodocus

We think that these dinosaurs used their long necks to munch on the tops of trees, like giraffes do today. Some scientists think that Brontosaurus and Diplodocus could even stand up on their back legs when they wanted to. That would make them able to nibble on leaves 40 or 50 feet in the air—more than twice as high as a giraffe can reach.

Tyrannosaurus (tuh-ran-uh-SAWR-us) looked like the meanest meat-eater in the world. Its name means "tyrant lizard," because it was supposed to be the terrible king of the terrible meat-eating dinosaurs. It stood almost 20 feet high, and its huge jaws were lined with sharp 7-inch teeth.

But Tyrannosaurus and the other meat-eaters had a pretty hard time getting a meal. The other dinosaurs didn't just sit around waiting to become lunch. They fought back.

Ankylosaurus (ang-KILE-o-sawr-us) probably didn't spend much time hiding from Tyrannosaurus. On its back it had heavy plates of bone. At the end of its tail was a chunk of bone that it could swing like a heavy club.

Triceratops's (try-SAIR-uh-tops) head had three sharp horns and a broad shield. Charging into Tyrannosaurus, it could probably knock over and even kill the mighty hunter.

And the big plant-eaters like Brontosaurus were so much bigger than the meat-eaters that they could smash them with their long tails or stomp them with their huge feet.

It was enough to make a hungry Tyrannosaurus think about eating a nice tasty tree.

Hypacrosaurus

One group of dinosaurs had beaks that looked
like duck beaks, so those dinosaurs were
nicknamed duckbills. Many duckbills had strangely
shaped heads. Some had long spikes. Others, like
Hypacrosaurus (high-pa-crow-SAWR-us), had thin
bony crests. Parasaurolophus (pair-a-sawr-a-LOFF-us)
had a bony tube rising behind its skull.

Parasaurolophus

Some scientists have noticed that these crests and tubes were hollow and were connected to the duckbills' noses. This means that the hollow tubes could have worked like the "slide" on a trombone. (The slide is what allows the trombone to make its ringing sound.) When a bunch of duckbill "trombone-heads" got together to hoot and snort, it must have made quite a noise!

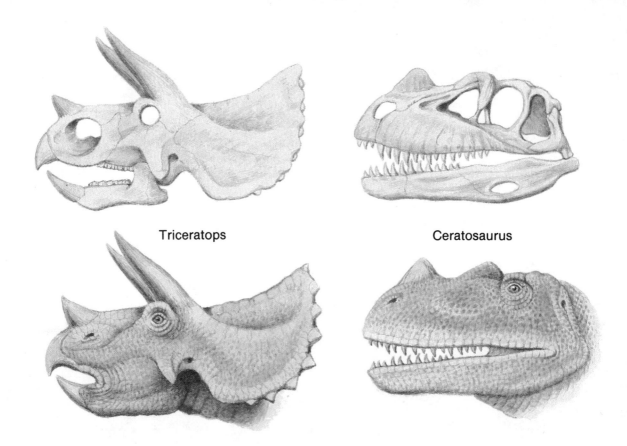

Triceratops

Ceratosaurus

Dinosaur teeth were very different from your teeth. Some dinosaurs had flat teeth and some had pointed teeth. One dinosaur, Heterodontosaurus (het-er-o-don-tow-SAWR-us), even had both kinds of teeth. But whatever sort of teeth a dinosaur had, it would lose them all the time.

A meat-eater's teeth broke off when it bit into bones, and a plant-eater's teeth were worn away when it chewed tough plants. But no matter how many teeth dinosaurs lost, they always had plenty more.

Unlike people, dinosaurs always had new teeth growing up under each tooth in their mouths. So when they lost a tooth, there was always another one ready to take its place. And even if the old tooth wasn't torn out or ground down, it would be pushed out by the new tooth growing up under it and would fall out all by itself.

Ceratosaurus

Triceratops

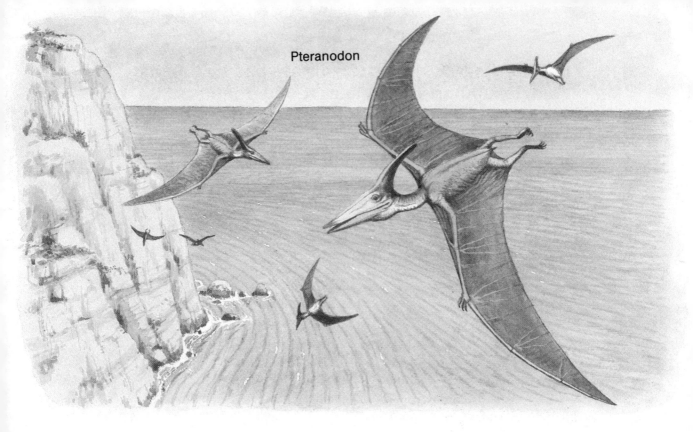
Pteranodon

You've probably noticed that *saur*, the word for "lizard," appears in many dinosaur names. That is because today's lizards are the animals that look most like dinosaurs did. Were dinosaurs big lizards? Not really. They were like lizards in some ways, but they were also a lot like birds.

How do we know? Some dinosaurs, like Pteranodon (ter-AN-o-don) and Quetzalcoatlus (KET-zahl-ko-AHT-los), probably flew. Quetzalcoatlus was a flying giant with wings 40 feet wide. Many dinosaurs also had bones that were like the bones of birds. And many of the plant-eaters probably had gizzards, too, which were special stomachs filled with stones that they swallowed.

What good were gizzards? They let the dinosaurs eat plants that were too tough for their teeth to chew. These dinosaurs bit off big pieces of plants and swallowed them. The rolling, grinding stones in their gizzards did the chewing.

Today, birds are the biggest group of animals with gizzards. Scientists think that the dinosaurs may have been the first animals with gizzards.

Quetzalcoatlus

There are no more dinosaurs. They're all gone.
Every single one of them died about 65 million
years ago.

What happened to them? We think that Earth
changed in some way and that the dinosaurs
couldn't live through it. One idea is that a huge rock
from outer space crashed into Earth. It threw huge
clouds of dust into the air. The dust clouds dimmed
the sun, and Earth became too cold for the
dinosaurs to live.

But it wasn't the first time that terrible things happened to the dinosaurs. Scientists have learned that dinosaurs were almost wiped out several times by accidents like this one. Each time, a few dinosaurs lived through it, and new kinds of dinosaurs grew up to live in the new conditions— until the last big accident that killed all the dinosaurs and made way for the other animals that took their place.

Because dinosaurs aren't around anymore, you might think they didn't really have what it takes to survive. But the dinosaurs ruled Earth for a long, long time—about 130 million years. That's twice as long as the many kinds of living mammals have been around. What are mammals? Most of the animals you know best are mammals: dogs, cats, cows, horses, monkeys. You are a mammal, as are all people.

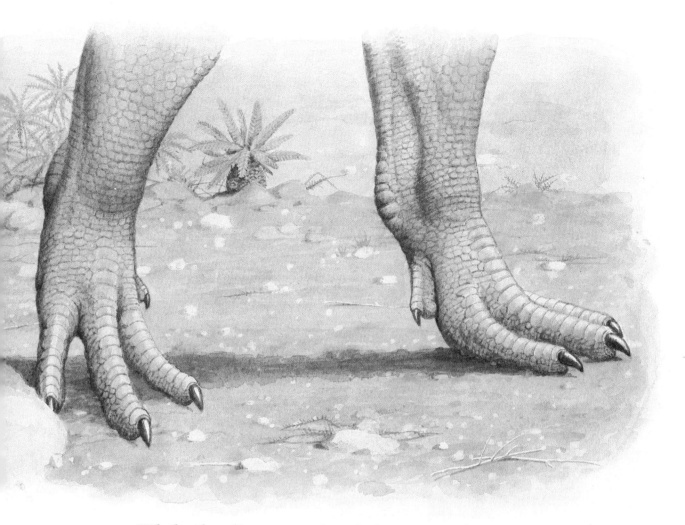

While the dinosaurs lived they were the biggest animals on Earth. Some mammals, like Phascolotherium (fas-ko-lo-THER-e-um), lived in dinosaur times, too. But as long as the dinosaurs lived, no mammal grew to be bigger than a cat.

Today, all of the biggest animals on Earth are mammals, like elephants, whales, giraffes, and gorillas. The animals that are most like dinosaurs—lizards and birds—are pretty small.

If you found a few bones lying on the ground, could you tell very much about the animal they came from? Maybe not, but that's how scientists find out about dinosaurs. They study old bones, old rocks, old plants, and old footprints. After studying, thinking, and talking to other scientists, they make guesses. The guesses are pretty good ones, because the scientists work hard—but they're still guesses.

Because we're guessing, our ideas about dinosaurs are changing all the time. Scientists get new ideas as they find more bones and continue to study old ones. When other scientists hear about a new idea, they usually say, "No, it couldn't be."

But they also study the new idea. And after a while they may say, "Well, maybe it *might* have been like that."

Then they study some more, and sometimes they are able to say, "You know, it probably *was* like that after all!"

That's how we figure out what dinosaurs were like, how they lived, what they ate, and why they all died.

Maybe you can help. If you really like to learn about dinosaurs, perhaps you'll become a dinosaur scientist and join the guessing game. And maybe you'll be the one to find something different or think up a new idea about dinosaurs. After all, *somebody* has to make the next dinosaur discovery!